LIFE AND TEACHING OF SAINT SERAPHIM OF SAROV

by N. Puretzki
and
the Monastery of Sarov

Gozalov Books
The Hague

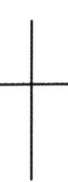

This book has the blessing of
Monsignor Simon, Archbishop of Brussels and Belgium
and temporarily of The Hague and the Netherlands

© Gozalov Books, The Hague, 2007
ISBN: 978-90-812765-2-8
Telephone/Fax: +31- 70-352 15 65
E-mail: gozalovbooks@planet.nl

The English translation of a Russian book 'Преподобный Серафим Саровский' by N. Puretzki, Moscow, 1903. Saint Seraphim's Teaching was taken from the book 'Житие старца Серафима, Саровской обители иеромонаха, пустынножителя и затворника', a reprint edition by the Moscow Section of the National Trust for Preservation of Monuments, Moscow, 1991

Editors:
'The Life of Saint Seraphim': Robin Winckel-Mellsih
'The Teaching of Saint Seraphim': the Convent in the name of the Mother of God Portaïtissa at Trazegnies, Belgium
Translators: Guram Kochi and Marijcke Tooneman

Illustrations: Elena Obodova, Minsk, Beylorussia

Cover image: photo of the miracle-working icon of Saint Seraphim of Sarov, in the Church in the name of Saint Maria Magdalena, The Hague
Interior: 'Rossco Desktop Publishing', Amsterdam

All rights reserved. No part of this publication may be reproduced or transmitted in any form or by any means, electronic or mechanical, including photocopy and recording, or stored in a retrieval system, without the written permission of the publisher.

FOREWORD BY THE TRANSLATORS

The story about the life of Saint Seraphim of Sarov[1], the miracle-worker, was first printed by the Monastery of Sarov in 1893. It was then re-written by N. Puretzki and published by the printer I. D. Sytin in Moscow in 1903.
Saint Seraphim's Teaching was taken from the original edition of this book, which was reprinted in Moscow in 1991 by the Moscow Section of the National Trust for Preservation of Monuments.

The cover image is a photo of one of Saint Seraphim's miracle-working icons. This icon was presented to the Russian Orthodox Church in the name of Saint Mary of Magdala in The Hague by the last Russian Tzar, Nicolas II, a martyr and a saint; the reason being that this church was originally the domestic chapel of Queen Anna Paulowna, who was a member of the Royal Romanov House, and the wife of King, Willem II of the Netherlands. This icon has another particular characteristic: it is not a strictly formal representation of a saint, but one of the two portraits of Saint Seraphim.

The church also has in her possession part of the relics of Saint Seraphim, and pilgrims from all over Europe and Russia come to venerate them and to pray.
Saint Seraphim is one of the most venerated saints of Russia, and has greatly influenced the spiritual life, not only of the entire Russian clergy, but also of the thousands of laymen who were drawn to Christian mysticism.
Staretz[2] Seraphim has formulated in his teaching in simple words the purpose and the ways of Christian ascetic life, in order to make them understandable to all those seeking God.

FOREWORD BY THE TRANSLATORS

In future we will translate and publish more books about Christian Orthodox ascetics and mystics of Russia.

Guram Kochi and Marijcke Tooneman

The Hague, January 2008

Contents

Foreword by the Translators vi

The Life of Saint Seraphim 1
Prayer to Father Serafim 21
Endnotes 22

The Teaching of Saint Seraphim 23
1. On God 25
2. On Faith 26
3. On Hope 26
4. On love of God 27
5. On the fear of God 27
6. On renouncing the world 28
7. On silence 29
8. On heedfulness of oneself 30
9. On the care for the soul 33
10. With what should one nourish one's soul 34
11. On peace of soul 36
12. On preserving peace of soul 38
13. On feats 39
14. On the light of Christ 41
15. On tears 41
16. On repentance 42
17. On fasting 45
18. On guarding the mind 46
19. On verbosity 47
20. On discernment of what is in the heart 48
21. On illnesses 49
22. On almsgiving 49
23. On thoughts and impulses of the flesh 50
24. On patience and humility 52
25. On duties and love for one's neighbours 54
26. On not condemning one's neighbour
    and on forgiveness of insults 55

Contents

27. Against excessive care 57
28. On sadness 58
29. On despair 58
30. On the reasons why Jesus Christ came
    into the world 61
31. On the active and the contemplative life 62

THE LIFE OF SAINT SERAPHIM

In our faithless century, Staretz Seraphim was an unusual man and resembled the reincarnation of an ancient ascetic from the desert of Thebes, or from the caves of Kiev. All sorts of people, members of the gentry, simple folk and the rich and the poor, visited him in his cell and often prostrated themselves before the bent old man, dressed in an old shapeless garment. They entrusted their innermost secrets to him, their sorrows and needs, and lovingly accepted each word of his, filled with the life-giving warmth of blessing. The words of the Staretz, spoken from his narrow cell, will be spread around vast Russia for many centuries to come, and as beautiful seeds they will bring forth the fruit of good deeds.

The wordly name of Father Seraphim was Prohor, and he was born in 1759 in the city of Kursk[3], in Russia. His father, Isidor Moshnin, was a building contractor. He owned a brick factory and contracted various building jobs, including churches. A well-known church that he built, the Saint Sergii of Radonezh[4] Cathedral, is still to be found in the Kursk province. The design of this cathedral was made by the famous Italian architect Rastrelly, and the building was completed in 1778.

Isidor Moshnin passed away when Seraphim was just three years old and he was raised by his mother Agaphia, who was a pious woman. She attended church every Sunday, dedicated herself to charity work and the care of the helpless and poor. Prohor inherited her kind and sensitive heart, and Agaphia brought him up in the spirit of piety which influenced his life until his death. This was the most beneficial influence to determine the ethic codes of the future ascetic. Even as a child Prohor avoided the usual games of his contemporaries, and attended church services, prayed and listened with interest to the stories of the lives of the saints. There were several events in his life which show that the boy was under a special protection, and the first took place when Prohor was about seven years old.

The Life of Saint Seraphim

His father was building a large new church in the name of St. Sergi, in Kursk, by order of the parishioners. Their means were insufficient, and the building process was delayed. When the ground floor of the church was ready, Isidor Moshnin died and he requested that his wife finish the building of the church. Agaphia obeyed her husband's will and continued to supervise the building of the church. Four years after her husband had passed away, when Prohor was seven years old, Agaphia took him with her to the top of the scaffolding around the bell-tower, which was about 15 meters high. Prohor stumbled on a piece of wood and fell off the scaffold to the ground. Horrified, Agaphia rushed down, convinced that her little Prohor had fallen to his death, but instead she saw Prohor standing there quietly.

"Prohor, my dear, you are alive!" she cried, sobbing with joy and pressing her son, saved by a miracle, to her chest.

Soon afterwards another incident took place around the time when he started to learn to read and write, which made it clear that God was indeed protecting Prohor.

The ancient custom was that after learning the alphabet, a child had to learn to read from the Book of Hours, followed by the Psalter and other sacred books. Prohor read according to this old method, and diligently studied the sacred books, and the people around him were struck by the sharpness of his intelligence as he expressed the divine meaning of the Bible as if he were an adult. He was thought to be a very promising child, but his studies came to an abrupt halt, when, even though he was strongly built, he suddenly became so seriously ill that his mother lost all hope of his recovery. In the depth of his illness, Prohor saw, in a subtle dream, the most Holy Mother of God, who promised to come to him soon to heal him.   Prohor woke to see his mother weeping inconsolably beside his bed, and he told her about his vision which turned out to be prophetic. A few days later a religious procession carrying one of the miraculous icons of Kursk: The Mother of God of Kursk, passed Moshnin's house just as a downfall of rain started, and the priest decided to shorten the route and to go through the Moshnin's garden. Pious Agaphia thought that this was a sign for her, and with flaming faith in her heart, she took Prohor from his bed and took him outside to witness the icon. Prohor kissed the holy icon and felt better immediately, and soon after he recovered completely. And so the promise of the Mother of God to visit and heal him came true.

While recovering from his illness, Prohor returned to the studies of the Book of Hours and the Psalter, and also learned to write. Reading the Bible and the sacred books of the Old and New Testament had become his favourite pastime and kept him busy.

In the former times in Russia, children could attended classes only for a short while, and Prohor's mother too, did not allow him to study books for too long. She wanted to prepare him for some kind of practical activity and sent him to work in the shop of his elder brother, Alexey. Alexey traded in goods necessary to a peasant: ropes, straps, harnesses, yokes, etc. He was an experienced merchant and managed his business skilfully, and also enjoyed it. Prohor, however, had developed a distinct aversion to the merchant's business and he felt only attracted to those places where he would be able to gain spiritual treasure: eternal salvation. He attended the church service daily, without exception, and only here did his soul feel at home as daily life stifled him. During the week, because of his work, he could only attend the early morning worship and so he got up very early and after zealously praying in front of the icons at home, he hurried to church, to the temple of the living God, so as to offer his ardent prayers and thanksgivings. During the feast days, Prohor spent all his free time attending the church services so as to read the holy Scriptures and the Paterics[5]: the descriptions of the life of saints - the most important to our ancestors.

Sometimes the boy gathered his friends around him and told them about the treasures of the spiritual wisdom that he found in books. Although they listened to him gladly, his inner voice usually told him to withdraw from people and to meditate. Even in Prohor's early years he was able to glimpse the elevated ascetic spirit, and the fire of this spirit never extinguished in him, on the contrary, it often burned immensely bright in the course of his life. People from all over Russia, monks and laymen, knew of him and considered him to be their spiritual mentor, even though most of his life was spent in complete solitude, as he humbly carried the burden of the life of an ascetic. This ascetic spirit became especially strong after Prohor had several talks with one of 'God's fools in Christ', who lived in the streets of Kursk. This 'God's fool' regularly visited Prohor's parents, and they gave him food and shelter.

A true 'God's fool in Christ's ship', as it is called, is one of the most difficult and greatest of all the ascetic practices. A few especially zealous ascetics, stimulated by their love for God , got out of hand, and even though they looked mad, they still managed to retain a clear inner awareness. These chosen one's based their practice on the literal meaning of Christ's words: 'Do not care with your soul, what you eat or what you drink; and do not care with your body what clothes you wear; the soul is more important than the food, and the body is more important than the cloth.' (Matth. 6, 25). They were the true wanderers, the 'citizens of the heavenly fatherland' who had neither home nor any means of income. Through their words (often cryptic) and their conduct (often very odd) they were to their contemporaries a living reminder of the higher purposes of our existence. The 'God's fools for Christ,' boldly unmasked the rich and the mighty on earth, and consoled those who suffered; they tried to put right the fallen and support and protect the weak and helpless. They were deprived of everything and wandered, showing all Christians by the way they lived, that it is more important to care for the Heavenly Kingdom than for perishable, earthly goods. These were deliberate martyrs who were always trying to be 'dead' to the world, the flesh and the devil, in order to live in Christ.

By nature Prohor did not feel attracted to the earthly purposes and pleasures, and talks with the 'God's fool' made his feelings for the heavenly Spirit even stronger, and all the seeds in his soul, planted by his parents, the priest and the reading of ascetic literature, grew even stronger. His mind was engaged most of the time with the Holy Scripture or with an ardent prayer.

As the apostle Paulus said: "The Holy Spirit has put together in the Gospels everything which is necessary for the learning, for the unmasking, for the improvement of man, and for teaching him righteousness. A man of God should be perfect, and prepared to do any work for the sake of good." (2 Tim. 3, 16, 17). And so Prohor, by the mercy of God's blessing and with all his heart, tried to learn in the Holy Scripture so as to understand what God's will might be, and how he could realize the will of the heavenly Father in his life, and illuminate it by the light of His commands.

"Like a thirsty doe who seeks the water streams, so Prohor's soul aspired towards God, who is strong and alive." (Ps. 41, 2)

At the first stroke of the church bell, Prohor arrived in church and prayed, standing close to the doors. In his own house he had a secret place, where he sometimes prayed the whole night long, without sleeping. He humbly pleaded to God to give him the strength and intelligence to serve Him with his entire heart and soul, and to be included in the flock of the chosen ones. He pleaded for protection from worldly seductions, for help in his spiritual growth and the guidance of the Holy Spirit. His soul eliminated more and more the concrete things of this world, and he did not find them interesting. He clearly knew that he would not find in everyday life, full of temptations and barriers, that peaceful state of spirit which is necessary for an ascetic who strives for salvation. Prohor's soul, meek and loving, did not want anything but inner peace, and he sought solitude in untamed nature, far from people and their vanity, so as to find an intimate and constant contact with God. A fruitless, wild desert seemed to him a paradise!

These elevated, light and sacred feelings prompted him to take a decision of the heart, and Prohor revealed to his mother, humbly and sincerely, his innermost thoughts and wishes.

'My dear mother,' he said, 'I ask for your blessing so that I can retire to the cloister. In everyday life I feel consumed with anguish; perhaps it is Lord himself who calls me!'

'Yes, if you feel you have a vocation, then God will bless you and give you strength, and I will not stand in your way, I will not try to keep you with me,' his mother answered. She was a simple Russian woman, old and weak in her body, but strong in her faith and spirit. Even though she felt sorry that she had to part with her favourite son, she did not want to stop him realizing his dream.

Soon after, Prohor made his first step towards this goal and he acquired the necessary 'dismissal testimony[6]' from the city community. This was the first step in renouncing the world - his first visible step. In his soul Prohor had already renounced the pleasures of this world a long time ago.

The difficult hour of departure came, but Prohor loved God so much that he was determined to break the strong ties with his mother and relatives.

In the large living-room of their house, all the relatives and acquaintances of the Moshnin family came together. Prohor came into the room escorted by his sobbing mother, and all those present sat down for a moment, as it is done according to the old Russian custom, before a long parting. Then Prohor stood up, bowed before his mother and asked for her blessing. Still sobbing, his mother held out the icons of Christ and the Mother of God to him, and Prohor kissed them piously. Then his mother made the sign of the cross with a copper cross and gave it to Prohor. He put the cross on solemnly, and never took it off.

Prohor crossed himself, looking at the church, took his knapsack and a pilgrim's crook, and left resolutely, leaving behind his parental house, his mother, brother and sister whom he loved so much. He was just seventeen years old.

The destination of his pilgrimage was Kiev, the source of the Russian monastic life, and Prohor hoped to find contact there with the spirit of the ancient ascetics. In the Kitaevski Cloister he met an ascetic, called Dosiphei, a sagacious Staretz, full of God's grace. Dosiphey prophesized where Prohor's future ascetic practices would take place – the Cloister in Sarov. Prohor confessed his sins, received communion, bowed before the relics of the Pecherski saints[7] and went back to Kursk.

There he took final leave of his mother and went to Sarov. The Prior of the cloister, who was called Pahomi, received the youth cordially, as he immediately that Prohor had a true vocation for the monastic life. Prohor became one of the novices of the cloister and his mentor was Father Josef, who was the cloister's treasurer. His first work of penance was to clean the cell of Father Josef, and to carry out his orders. He also had to other works of penance, such as work in the cloister's bakery, in the prosfornja[8], and in the carpentry, and he also became the sexton and had to see to it that the monks woke up in time for morning prayer. Prohor was physically strong and vigilant and he worked zealously, he enjoyed being useful to the cloister and delighted his soul in prayers.

His physical obligations alternated between reading the Bible, studying the works of the church fathers and Chetji –Minei[9], written by Saint Dmitri of Rostov, and the stories of the lives of the saints made him want to follow their example. Prohor constantly prayed the Jesus prayer, full of humility and grievance for his sins. These practices, however, did not seem to be enough for Prohor and he desperately wanted a life in complete solitude.

The Cloister of Sarov was surrounded by a thick coniferous forest where a few monks lived. Prohor wanted to follow their example and his mentor gave him permission to retreat now and then into the thick of the forest and pray to God there. Prohor's humble character, his obedience with regard to the monastic rule, his irrepressible wish to pray, and his ardent faith in God gained him the favour of

THE LIFE OF SAINT SERAPHIM

all the monks. This was especially clear when he became seriously ill and could not get out of bed due to dropsy, and even the Prior himself was close to Prohor almost all of his free time. When the illness became worse, the doctor and the Prior suggested that Prohor let blood, and he answered: 'I have entrusted myself to the true physician of our souls and bodies, our Lord Jesus Christ and to his most pure Mother. However, if you love me then administer to me, the humble one, for God's sake, heavenly treatment.' The Prior held a nightly service and liturgy with prayers for Prohor's recovery. Prohor confessed his sins and received the sacraments, which his mentor Father Josef had offered to him, with deep faith in his heart. Soon after the communion Prohor had a vision: the most Holy Mother of God appeared before him surrounded by an indescribable light, escorted by the apostles John the Theologian, and Peter.

Prohor told his fellow ascetics about the vision a few years later and said that the most Holy Virgin pointed at him and said to the apostles: 'He is of our kind!' With these words She put her hand on his head, and suddenly a hole appeared in Prohor's side through which all the dampness escaped from his body, and he felt relieved. Within a few days he had recovered completely which greatly surprised the physicians and his brethren.

After Prohor's recovery, the Prior imposed on him his last penance as a novice: he had to travel to the surrounding towns and villages and collect money for the building of the new church. He also visited his native city Kursk, where he prayed on the grave of his mother who had passed away.

It was eight years since Prohor had left the mundane life behind him and had become a novice in the Cloister of Sarov. This period in the monastic life is called 'the time of ordeals', which signifies the period when it is decided whether the candidate is 'worthy of the angelic rank', as this is how the monks are considered in the heavenly hierarchy.

On the 13th August 1786, Prohor, at the age of twenty five, and in the prime of his life, took his monastic vows from Prior Pahomi and received the monastic name Seraphim, which means 'the fiery, or ardent', because the Prior and the other monks saw his flaming love of God in his heart and his zealous striving to live according to God's will. In the same year Seraphim became a deacon and the next six years of his life were spent worshipping continuously in the church. God seemed to give him strength, as Seraphim did not need much rest, and he often forgot to eat and left the church after the service regretting that he could not stay longer. Sometimes, during the service, he was able to see the angels who were serving and singing with the monks.

He received an especially remarkable vision during the liturgy on Maundy Thursday during the service. When the Gospels were taken from the alter he saw our Lord Jesus Christ in His image of the Son of Man in all His glory, shining brighter than the sun and surrounded by the heavenly hierarchies. Christ the Saviour walked above the ground from the west gates of the altar, stood still for a while above the pulpit, raised his hands and blessed the clergy and all those in the church.

Father Seraphim couldn't move or say a word during the vision, and he just stood by the pulpit, looking at something that only he could see. Two deacons took him by his arms and steered him to the altar where he stood transfixed in the heavenly vision of God's appearance.

The superiors of the cloister recognised that Father Seraphim's ascetic virtues were above the other brethren of the cloister, and recommended that he be initiated into the priesthood, and Archbishop Theophyl of the city of Tambov performed the ceremony. According to the other monks, Father Seraphim exercised the ascetic practices even more zealously after his initiation. He celebrated the Holy Liturgy and received the Sacraments with ardent love, faith and reverence every day. After the liturgy he performed various works of penance in the cloister, but in

THE LIFE OF SAINT SERAPHIM

the evening he retired to his favourite place, a remote cell in the forest where he spent his time praying. After several years Father Seraphim asked the Prior for his blessing to retire fully to his cell. The Prior gave him his blessing and Father Seraphim left the cloister and lived in a small hut in the forest.

Only God knows the many hardships which Father Seraphim had to undergo in the solitude of his ascetic hut. He had, however, struggled with the seductions of the flesh and with all worldly temptations since his childhood, and had won them, even before he became a monk. Now, however, besides the enemies he already knew, he had to wage the bitter and unending war with the most bold enemy of human salvation: the evil spirits, or 'spiritual lions'. These invisible servants of darkness are the worst enemies of an ascetic. They shoot their poisons arrows and hinder his Path to the heavens. Father Seraphim won all these battles with the help of God's blessing, which protected him from the demons who tried everything in order to divert him from his Path. Father Seraphim was once praying in his hut at night, when a large number of evil spirits attacked his hut. Some in the form of snakes, crawled next to his feet, threatening to bite him; another flew nearby him, threatening to drink his blood, while others tried to scare him with their wild wails and hellish anger. As soon as they had disappeared another menace arrived, making his wretched hut shake and almost fall apart, and these devil's threats could be heard from afar. As soon they had disappeared another arrived, in the form of a coffin. The coffin's lid fell open and the dead, covered with a white shroud, arose.

How much spiritual strength must a man carry in order to ward off these enemy attacks, and once more feel the stillness and the much longed for peace of the soul? For three long years Father Seraphim knelt on a stone for many hours, praying to the Mother of God, asking Her for protection.

With Her help Father Seraphim could fearlessly endure all these hellish attacks and the horror of their threats, and by stringent fasting and incessant prayers, he won over these frightening delusions by pronouncing: 'Let God resurrect and let his enemies scatter...' With these words they disappeared like smoke and the malice of the bad spirits melted from the fire of Seraphim's prayer like wax.

Devils often attacked Father Seraphim taking the form of blood-thirsty wild beasts, just as Saint Sergi of Radonez and Saint Anthony the Great had experienced such attacks in their times. As he warded off these vicious attacks, he no longer feared the living predatory animals of the forest. A large packs of hungry wolves scoured for food near his wretched hut, and he was often visited by the even more formidable inhabitants of the forest: bears.

More then once the compassionate hermit shared his last piece of bread with them, training himself even more to endure the hardships of the ascetic life.

All these ordeals and horrifying attacks had only one purpose: the devil wanted to chase Father Seraphim from his cell, so that he would discontinue his ascetic practices. When Father Seraphim disgraced the devil, despite all the devil's attacks, his enemy tried to harm him indirectly, through evil people.

Once while Father Seraphim was chopping wood near his hut, three unknown peasants came to him and brutally demanded his money. 'I do not take money from anyone,' he answered. One of the peasants ran towards him and tried to hit him, but miraculously fell to the ground before Father Seraphim. The other two became frightened, but Father Seraphim, though he was very strong and had an axe, said the words of Christ to himself: "Those who take the sword will perish by the sword.' Then he put his axe down, crossed his arms and asked the robbers what they wanted. The peasant who had fallen, grabbed the axe and hit Father Seraphim's head with the back of it. Blood gushed from his mouth and ears, and he fell to the ground.

The peasants, while kicking him, dragged him to his cell, tied him up with a rope and left him there thinking that he would certainly die. Then they ran to his cell hoping to find money, but they only found icons and a couple of potatoes. They came to their senses and felt horrified by what they had done and ran away.

Father Seraphim, however, was only unconscious, and when he regained consciousness he untied himself, prayed to God and thanked Him for this suffering, and asked Him to forgive his offenders and went to the cloister. As he could barely walk, he reached the cloister only the next morning, covered in dry blood, his clothes torn to pieces, and the doctors who examined him found that his scull was fractured, several ribs were broken, his chest was hurt and he had several serious wounds on his body. While they were discussing in Latin what they should do, Father Seraphim fell asleep and had a vision.

The most Holy Mother of God appeared before him in all Her glory, accompanied by the apostles John the Theologian and Peter. She came to his bed and said, looking at the physicians: "You need not toil, he is of My kind!" When father Seraphim woke up he would not accept the treatment that the physicians offered. He felt better the same day and got out of bed, though he did remain in the cloister for five months until he had completely recovered and then returned to his hut.

Soon after the police established the guilt of the peasants who tried to rob him, and Father Seraphim said to the Prior of the cloister and to the landlord whose serfs were the same peasants, that if they were punished he would leave Sarov forever and would go and live elsewhere, very far away. The villains were forgiven, because of Father Seraphim's pleading, but their houses were burned to ashes soon after. They went to visit him to repent their sins, begging him to plead for them.

Soon after all this happened, Father Seraphim decided, as if seclusion was not enough, to undertake another great ascetic practice: the vow of silence. He closed the doors of his hut to visitors, who came to him regularly to ask for his prayers, and if he met someone in the forest he would throw himself to the ground with his face downwards and he would lie like that until the person went away.

A specially appointed monk from the cloister, brought food to his hut once a week, which was especially difficult in the winter as there were no path to the hut and the ground was often covered with deep snow. When the monk reached the hut, he would enter, say a prayer, bow before Father Seraphim, and then return to the cloister.

He lived like this for several years, coming to the cloister only to receive Holy Communion. His legs, however, were damaged after three years of kneeling on stone, and he became so ill that he could not walk the distance. The Prior of the cloister ordered him to return to the cloister and Father Seraphim obeyed.

The ascetic Father Seraphim thus returned to the cloister on the 12th May 1810, after fifteen years of solitude, and went straight to the church of the hospital where the Prior and the monks welcomed him with great joy. They were, however, surprised the next day, when, after Holy Communion, Father Seraphim returned to his cell without exchanging a word to anyone and locked himself up in his cell where he remained alone. There was nothing in his cell except an icon, an oil lamp which burned before it, and a wooden stump which served as a chair. For the sake of self-flagellation, he wore a cast-iron cross of about 25 cm long under his clothes. These were the same clothes that he wore while in solitude: a long white loose overall. His food consisted only of oats and chopped cabbage, and he only drank water which was brought to him regularly by one of the monks who would leave it outside the door. Father Seraphim would cover himself with a piece of cloth and would crawl on his knees, so that nobody could see him, to get his food and water. It often happened that both the food and water remained untouched, and the monk-servant took it away assuming that the ascetic Father Seraphim had deprived himself of food once more.

During his seclusion Father Seraphim received the Sacraments every Sunday and on church feast days. The Sacraments were brought to his cell after the early liturgy, and so as not to forget death, he received permission to place a coffin, that he had hollowed out himself from an oak trunk, in the small entrance of his cell. He used to say to his fellow monks: 'I beseech thee, brethren, to bury me in my coffin.'

Staretz Seraphim had spent about five years in strict solitude when he finally opened the door of his cell to other monks, though the ascetic did not break his vow of silence, not even to the Bishop of Tambov, who visited the Cloister of Sarov and wanted to meet him. The Bishop, escorted by the Prior of the cloister, Nifont, came to Seraphim's cell and found the door locked from inside. They knocked and Prior Nifont announced loudly that the Bishop had arrived and wished to meet him, but the ascetic did not reply.

'With your blessing my Lord, can't we remove the door?' asked the Prior. 'I am not sure if Staretz is still alive.' The Bishop, however, thought it might be a sin to break open the cell and went away.

Father Seraphim broke his ten year solitude ten days later, when the most Holy Mother of God appeared before him again and instructed him to open the door of his cell for those seeking his advice or asking for his prayers.

Father Seraphim received both brethren and laymen in his cell thereafter, and taught them gladly and lovingly about Christian life. He had that special gift of love and humility, and no matter who came to him, he would kiss them, bow down before them, and while giving his blessing he sometimes kissed the hand of his visitor. Some visitors heard a denunciation from him, but even that was made in a meek, cordial voice. Father Seraphim tried to wake them from their sleeping conscience, but he did it in such an indirect way that they were not even aware that his denunciation was directed at them. During the last ten years of his life, Father Seraphim was visited by more than 2000 people daily, and all of them felt his love for them.

Even people with closed hearts shed streams of tears while talking to Staretz.

There were always many burning candles before the icons in Father Seraphim's cell and his visitors often brought candles and oil, sometimes money, which he sometimes accepted. When they asked why there are so many candles, he would answer: 'I put a candle before the holy icon for those who trust me. If this candle falls, then it is a sign that the person before me has lapsed into deadly sin. I then genuflect before the grace of God, and plead for their soul.'

Thousands of testimonies testify to Father's Seraphim sagacity, many of them remarkable. In 1829 a gentleman wanted to marry a woman of lower standing, against the will of his parents, and decided to turn to Father Seraphim to gain his favour, as he knew that his parents respected him very much and would not question his affirmation. He prepared himself with all kinds of arguments, justifying his decision, even with quotations from the Holy Bible, and went to visit Father Seraphim. To his astonishment, the first thing he heard when he entered Seraphim's cell, was the name of the woman he wanted to marry and all his arguments and quotations from the Holy Bible that he had prepared in advance to convince Staretz. Speechless he fell on his knees before Staretz. Father Seraphim helped him to get up and said: "God and Mother of God disapprove of your intentions and you will not marry her." The marriage indeed did not take place, and after returning home the man told his parents that before meeting the ascetic he did not believe that there were any righteous men, but his visit to Staretz Seraphim had convinced him of the opposite.

A priest from Nizhni Novgorod, whose mother became suddenly very ill when he was a child, relates the story of how his father, who was a deacon at the village church, went by foot to Father Seraphim, at the Cloister of Sarov, 25 kilometres away from his village, as he believed that only Father Seraphim could save his wife. When he arrived at the cloister, he was told that Staretz was in his remote hut in the forest, and he rushed off there. He met Seraphim half-way, and Father Seraphim held out his hands towards him and exclaimed: 'Oh, a troubled man comes to me. People do awful things to each other!' When the deacon wanted to talk about his problem, Father Seraphim interrupted him and said: 'I know about your troubles.' He took the deacon's right hand and said: 'Repeat after me: 'Lord, I believe and profess that you are the true Christ, the Son of the living God, who came into the world." He did not continue the prayer, but repeated this first sentence three times. Then he told the deacon about God's mercy towards man, and about the hope for God's grace. The cloister bells rang, announcing the nightly service and Father Seraphim blessed the deacon and said: 'Go to the cloister and stand throughout the entire service, and after the service go home, do not stay in the cloister tonight as your family needs you. God will send a physician to your wife, there is one who lives not far away from you, and your wife will be healed.'

'But who is this physician', asked the deacon.

'Go to the service,' Father Seraphim repeated, 'and God will send a physician.'

'Tell me at least where he lives!' pleaded the deacon.

'Go and join the service,' repeated Father Seraphim, 'and God will send physician.'

The deacon stood throughout the entire service, deep into the night, and obeying the orders of Father Seraphim he returned home through the forests and fields and was not afraid of wild animals or robbers as he felt the protection of Father Seraphim. When he arrived home and told all those gathered there of Father Seraphim's words, someone remembered a peasant woman in the neighbouring village, who could heal with herbs. She was quickly brought in and she administered a tea with special herbs to the sick woman. The woman fell asleep a few times for a short while, and each time she woke, she received another sip of tea. Finally she slept for a few hours, and when she woke up she was healed. And so Father's Seraphim prediction came true!

Father Seraphim also had the gift of healing. He used to anoint sick people with oil from the oil lamp which burned before his most beloved icon of the Mother of God. The name of the icon 'The Tenderness', was called by Father Seraphim 'Joy beyond any joy', and when asked why he anointed sick people, he would answer: 'We read in the Holy Scripture that the apostles anointed sick people and many of them were healed, and who other than the apostles could be a better example for us?' Many of those whom Father Seraphim anointed were healed, and a serf even recovered his sight.

A rich landowner by the name of Mantorov, became seriously ill and the doctors could not establish the cause of his illness and because their treatments had no effect he was forced to leave military service. He settled in his manor house, called Noutch, situated 40 kilometers from the Cloister of Sarov. Rumours of Father Seraphim reached him and he travelled to Sarov. His illness had already progressed so far that he could not walk, and three of his serfs had to carry him to Father Seraphim's cell. Father Seraphim asked him three times: 'Do you believe without doubt in God?' And each time Mantorov answered: "I believe without doubt'. Staretz anointed parts of Mantorov's body and he became well and could leave the cell, walking without assistance.

He used water from a spring not far from the cloister to heal, ordering those seeking recovery, even with open wounds, to pour water from the spring over themselves. Many were healed and all were relieved from their diseases.

In the last years of his earthly life, he often repeated: 'Soon I will no longer be here, my end is near!' On Sunday January 1st, 1833, Father Seraphim came to the cloister church in the name of Saint Zosima and Savvati[10]. He placed candles before each icon, something which he had never done before, and received communion. After the liturgy he took leave of all the monks in the church and kissed and blessed them all, consoling them: 'Go on working for salvation, do not get depressed, keep vigil, today the wreaths are being prepared for us in heaven.' His body looked exhausted, but his spirit was vigilant, serene and joyful.

That same evening a monk called Paul, whose cell was close to Father Seraphim's, heard Staretz singing the Easter psalms: 'Having seen the resurrection of Christ...' 'Be blessed, oh new Jerusalem...', 'The great and the most sacred Easter, Christ...'

On the morning of the 2nd of January, Paul who left his cell to join the early morning liturgy, smelt burning near the cell of Father Seraphim. He said a short prayer, as did all the visitors of Seraphim and knocked on the door. There was no reply and the door was locked from inside. Paul walked out onto the front steps and beckoning to a few monks who were heading to church, said to them: 'Fathers and brethren! I smell a strong smell of burning coming from the cell of Father Seraphim, Staretz has probably left for his hut.' One of them, a novice called Anickita, rushed to Father Seraphim's cell and broke the door down. They could see a small fire and the monks gathered some snow and put out the fire. What was burning were linen cloths and books, which had been given to Father Seraphim by pilgrims. From the light of a candle they could see that Staretz stood on his knees before the lectern in his white loose overall, with his head bowed and his arms crossed on his chest. The oil lamp before the icon of the Mother of God called 'Tenderness' burnt, and on the lectern lay a prayer book with which he held his service to the veneration of the Mother of God. The monks thought that Staretz had fallen asleep and cautiously tried to wake him up, but in vain. Staretz, the ascetic Seraphim, had left this world.

The Life of Saint Seraphim

Prayer to Father Serafim

O, divine Father Seraphim,
The great miracle worker of Sarov and the one who helps all those who seek your aid and support.
No-one during the days of your earthly life, parted from you without being granted spiritual wealth and consolation, many enjoyed your sweet countenance and the sound of your gentle admonitions. You have shown the great gift of clairvoyance and of healing the feeble and sick souls and bodies.
When God summoned you from your earthly labour to a heavenly repose, your love still remained with us, and it is not possible to recall all your many miracles - they are as many as the stars in the sky! You appear everywhere in our land to God's people and heal them.
Inspired by this, we call upon you: O most serene and meek servant of God, endowed with a bold prayer to Him,
Offer up your prayers, filled with the strength of goodness, to the Lord God of Hosts, so that He will grant us everything that we need in this life for our salvation, let Him guard us from sin and let Him teach us true repentance,
So that we can enter the eternal Heavenly Kingdom, where you shine now in your everlasting glory, and sing there of the Trinity, the source of life, together with all the Saints, forever. Amen

ENDNOTES

1 Sarov: a small Russian town, about 200 km from the city of Nizhny Novgorod on the Volga.

2 Staretz: literal translation of 'an old, venerable man'. The meaning in the Russian orthodox tradition is 'spiritual mentor, or adviser'.

3 Kursk: a small city in central Russia.

4 Sergii of Radonezh: one of the most venerated saints of Russia, the founder of the Trinity Cloister in Zagorsk, not far from Moscow. Sergii of Radonezh was considered to be the Prior of all the Russian monks.

5 Pateric: a collection of the biographies of Christian ascetics and saints.

6 Dismissal testimony: in order to join a cloister in those times, special permission was needed, literally called 'dismissal testimony'.

7 Pecherski saints: is derived from the name 'Pecherskaja Lavra'. This was the first cloister in Kiev, which was the breeding-ground of the Russian Orthodox, Christian ascetics.

8 Prosfora: small round loaves used in the liturgical sacraments.

9 Chetji-Minei: the life-work of the Saint Dmitiri of Rostov, a collection of biographies of all the Christian saints.

10 Saint Zosima and Saint Savvati: the founders of a network of cloisters on the Solovetzki islands, in the north of Russia.

The Teaching of Saint Seraphim

1. On God

God is a fire which warms and makes glowing the hearts and the inner of man. Thus when we would feel cold in our hearts, which comes from the devil as the devil is cold, we must appeal to God. When God will come He will warm our hearts with perfect love not only for Him but for our neighbours also. The warmth will drive away the cold of the devil who hates what is good.

When asked, the Holy Fathers instructed: seek God but do not ask where He lives.

Where God is, there is no evil. Everything which comes from God is peaceful and useful, and leads man to self-reproach and humility.

God treats us lovingly not only when we do good things, but also, when we insult Him with our sins and call His fire upon us. It is incredible how long He tolerates our lawlessness! And it is incredible how merciful He is even when He punishes us!

Do not call God 'just', Saint Isaac says, as His just judgement is not to be seen in your deeds. It is true that David names Him just and righteous, but His Son had shown us that God is more benevolent and merciful. How can we say that He is just? We were sinners, and Christ died for us. (Isaac the Syrian, 90)

In the measure that man improves himself during his earthly life according to God's will, and follows Him, God will reveal His countenance to him when the age of truth comes. For when the righteous experience here on earth His contemplation, they see His image as if in a mirror, but in the age of truth they will receive the revelation of the truth.

If you do not know God, then it is impossible that love for Him will awaken in you. You cannot love God, if you have not seen Him. Seeing God comes sometimes from learning to know Him for contemplation does not precede knowledge about God

Do not reason about God's works when your stomach is satiated: there cannot possibly be any truthful knowledge about God's mysteries when the stomach is full.

2. On Faith

First and foremost man should believe in God, as 'He is, and those seeking Him are rewarded' (Heb., 11, 6)
Faith is, according to the teaching of Saint Antioch, the beginning of our union with God: a true believer is a stone of the temple of God, which is meant for the building of God the Father; this stone was lifted up by the power of Jesus Christ, that is by His cross and with the help of a rope, that is the grace of the Holy Spirit.
'Faith is dead without deeds' (Jac.2, 26). The deeds of faith are as follows: love, peace, all-enduring patience, mercy, humility, carrying one's own cross, and a life according to the commandments of the Spirit. Only such a faith is considered to be the true one. The true faith cannot be fruitless: one who truly believes will do good deeds unfailingly.

3. On Hope

All those who have a firm hope in God, are elevated to Him and they become illuminated by the radiance of the eternal light.
If man does not care excessively for himself, because he is consumed by his love for God and by good deeds and he knows that God will take care of him, then such a hope is a true and wise hope. However if man counts on himself and his virtues only, and prays to God for help only when unforeseen troubles befall him and he cannot find means to avoid them and he hopes for God's help, then such a hope is false and in vain.
True hope comes from only seeking the kingdom of God, when the seeker firmly believes that all the earthly needs of this temporary life will be satisfied.

The heart cannot be at peace until it has acquired such kind of hope. This is exactly the kind of hope which pacifies the heart and brings it joy. This is exactly the kind of hope about which the most holy lips of our Saviour said: 'Come unto me, all ye that labour and are heavy laden, and I will give you rest.'(Matth., 11, 28), that is, set your hope on Me, and you will find consolation in your labours and fears.

In the Gospel by St. Luke it is said about Simeon: 'And it was revealed unto him by the Holy Ghost, that he should not see death, before he had seen the Lord's Christ.' (Lk., 2, 26). The Righteous Simeon kept his hope alive, he was awaiting to see the longed-for Saviour of the world. And when he received Him joyfully in his arms, he said: 'Lord, now lettest thou thy servant depart in peace, according to thy word for mine eyes have seen thy salvation.'

4. ON LOVE OF GOD

He who acquires perfect love of God, lives this earthly life as if he were not here. For he considers himself to be a stranger in the visible world, who is patiently waiting for the invisible one. He is filled completely with the love of God and has renounced other attachments.

He who loves himself cannot love God. And he who does not love himself because of his love for God, loves God truly. He who loves God truly considers himself a wanderer and a stranger on this earth, as he longs for God and his soul and mind are focused on contemplating Him only.

A soul which is full of love for God will not fear the prince of the air even at the moment of its parting from the body. Considering the earth as a foreign land, such a soul will fly up, accompanied by Angels, to its homeland.

5. ON THE FEAR OF GOD

He who is determined to follow the path of inner vigilance must first of all have the fear of God, which is the source of wisdom. Let the words of the prophet: 'Serve the Lord with fear, and rejoice with trembling.'(Ps.2, 11) be always imprinted on his mind.

He must follow his path with utmost cautiousness and reverence in regard to all that is sacred, and not carelessly. Otherwise a terrifying sentence of God might be applied to him: 'Cursed be he that doeth the work of the Lord deceitfully,.' (Jer., 48, 10)

Reverential cautiousness is required because the sea (that is man's heart with all its thoughts and desires, which should be purified by means of mindfulness) is enormous: 'So is this great and wide sea, wherein are things creeping innumerable,' (Ps. 103, 25): that is, many and many idle, unjust and impure thoughts, coming to us from evil spirits, have their seat there.

'Fear God,' the Wise one says, 'and keep His commandments.' Observing His commandments you will do everything you do in the right way and you will always do the right thing. For, fearing God, you will do everything well, as you love Him. And do not be afraid of the devil: he who fears God will conquer the devil, for the devil has not power over such a person.

There are two kinds of fear: if you do not want to do evil, then fear God and restrain yourself from doing evil; and if you want to do good, then fear God and do good.

However nobody is able to acquire the fear for God until he has freed himself from daily worries. When the mind becomes free from worries then it is driven by the fear of God and it aspires to Gods Grace.

6. On renouncing the world

The fear of God can be acquired when a man, having renounced all that is of this world, focuses all his thoughts and feelings and immerses himself completely in the contemplation of God and the feeling of bliss which was promised to the saints.

It is impossible to renounce the world completely and to enter the state of spiritual contemplation as long as one remains in the world. For as long as passions are raging, one cannot acquire peace of soul. However the passions will not subside as long as we are surrounded by the objects which arouse them. In order to obtain perfect passionlessness and a perfect silence of the soul, man should meditate a lot on spiritual subjects and pray a lot. How would it ever be possible then to give oneself totally to the peaceful contemplation of God, to learn His law and ascend to Him on the wings of ardent prayer, while remaining amidst the incessant noise of fighting passions? The world is seized by evil.

The soul cannot love God sincerely without liberating itself first from the world. For the worldly involvement of the soul is, according to Saint Antioch, like a cover.

If we, he says also, live in a foreign town, which is far away from our own town, and if we know where our native town is, then why do we linger in that strange town and prepare the fields and build the houses there? And how will we be able to sing our song to the Lord while imprisoned in a foreign land? The world is an alien place, the domain of the prince of this century.

7. ON SILENCE

Saint Barsanuphius teaches: as long as the ship is sailing in the sea it is liable to troubles and storms; and when the ship has reached a quiet and peaceful harbour, it does not fear troubles and sorrows and storms, but stays in the stillness of the harbour. It is the same with you, oh monk: as long as you are amongst other people, expect sorrows and troubles and intrusions of the 'thought streams' of others, and when you enter silence and seclusion you have nothing to fear anymore. (Bars. Answer 8, 9)

Perfect silence is that very cross on which man should crucify himself with all his passions and lusts. However, note that Christ, our Lord, had endured first a great number of abuses and insults and only after that He ascended His cross. It is the same with us, monks, we will not be able to enter perfect silence and to cherish the hope of acquiring the perfection of the saints, if we do not endure suffering (and burdens) together with Christ. For, as the Apostle says: 'If we suffered together with Him, we will share His glory.' (Bars. Answer 342)

The one who took a vow of silence should always remember for what purpose he did it, so that his heart would not become distracted by something else.

8. On heedfulness of oneself

He who follows the path of heedfulness should not trust only on his heart, but should verify everything that is in his heart and all his life with God's law and with the lives of those who strove zealously to obtain piety, having followed, in their times, the same path. It is a convenient way to protect oneself from the evil one and to see the truth more clearly.

The mind of the man who follows the path of inner heedfulness is like a guard, like a vigilant keeper of the inner Jerusalem. Standing on the height of spiritual contemplation it watches through the eyes of purity the hostile powers which try to sneak into the soul and to nestle themselves there, as it was said by the Psalmist king David: 'and mine eye hath seen his desire upon mine enemies' (Ps. 53, 7). Neither the devil, which is 'like a roaring lion, seeking to swallow everybody' (1 Pt., 5, 8) nor 'the wicked bend their bow, they make ready their arrow upon the string, that they may privily shoot at the upright in heart.' (Ps. 10, 2) can hide themselves from these eyes.

According to the teaching of the Holy Fathers every man is accompanied by two angels: one angel is the good one and another one is the evil one. The angel of good is quiet, meek and silent. When he enters man's heart he converses with the heart about truth, purity, honesty, serenity, good deeds and virtues. When you feel this in your heart then obviously this is the Angel of truth who visited you. The evil spirit is bitterly witty, cruel and mad. When he enters your heart you will recognize him through his deeds. (Anthony, Word 61)

Pay heed to yourself, beloved, says Isaac the Syrian. Keep yourself busy with incessant inner work, pay heed to the sorrows which befall you and to your cell where you live in the monastery, and to the subtleness of your mind and the roughness of your understanding, and to the duration of your silence and to many medical treatments: these are the temptations, which sometimes are provided by the true Doctor for the sake of healing the inner man, and, sometimes, by devils. These treatments are sometimes hard labour and illnesses, and sometimes terrifying thoughts which come out of your soul and are fearful reminders of what will await you at the end; and sometimes there come inner warmth, full of grace and sweet tears and spiritual joy and others of this kind. Can you see clearly, in all these circumstances that your sore began to heal and skin to grow? Make a mark in your mind and examine yourself regularly and incessantly and see which of your passions have become weaker, according to you? Which passions are exterminated and have left you in peace, which passions have started to subside because your soul is becoming healthier and not because of the fact that the causes of these passions are not there? Which passions have you learned to conquer by your reason, and not only by depriving yourself from the cause of these passions?

Pay also heed to yourself, whether you can see that there is healthy flesh, that is, peace of soul, which grows in your decaying sore? Which passions attack you constantly and swiftly and what are the intervals between their attacks; are these bodily or spiritual passions or complex, mixed passions? Do they enter your memory as something weak or strong? Do they attack your soul like mighty ones or like sneaking thieves? How does your inner king, your mind, the ruler of the feelings, respond: does it join the battle when the passions attack it and exhaust them by its strength, or is it not skilled to distinguish the passions and does not work on them at all? Which passions are old and which passions just come? Do they manifest themselves in vivid images or without them, just like a feeling; or, do they appear just in your memory, without causing a turbulence in you, thoughts about them and response in your soul? This is how you can measure the degree of your soul's health. (Isaac the Syrian, Word 45)

Therefore such a person who pays heed to himself, following the teaching of the divine Paul, 'takes the whole armour of God, that he may be able to withstand in the evil day and…to stand' (Eph. 6, 13). By these arms and with the help of God's grace he wards off the visible consequences and wins over the invisible fighters. We see such an example of keeping vigil spiritually in the story of Job the longsuffering, whom the Church praises with the following words: 'though the pillar of his body was lacerated, the treasure of his spirit could not be stolen as the soul of the chaste one was armed' (Troparion of 6th May).

The one who follows this path should not listen to rumours which can cause idle and empty thoughts and memories in his mind, but he must pay heed to himself. It is especially necessary on this path to restrain oneself from paying attention to other pursuits, do not think and do not talk about them, following the instructions of king David: 'Concerning the works of men, by the word of thy lips I have kept me from the paths of the destroyer' (Ps. 16, 4) but to plead God: 'cleanse thou me from secret faults. Keep back thy servant also from presumptuous sins; let them not have dominion over me: then shall I be upright, and I shall be innocent from the great transgression.'. (Ps. 19, 13, 14)

In order to preserve your heedfulness vigilant, it is necessary to retire inside yourself as the Lord says: 'and salute no man by the way.' (Lk., 10, 4), that is do not talk when it is not necessary, unless someone runs after you hoping to hear a useful instruction from you for his salvation.

When you meet on your way elders or brethren, greet them by a bow keeping your eye looking downwards.

9. On the care for the soul

Man in regard to his body is like a burning candle. Just like a candle is burnt out after a while man will die one day. However his soul is immortal and therefore we should care more for our soul than for our body . 'For what is a man profited, if he shall gain the whole world, and lose his own soul? or what shall a man give in exchange for his soul? ' (Math. 16, 26). As it is known nothing in this world can be worthy of the soul. And if the soul by itself alone is more precious than the whole world and the worldly kingdom, then the heavenly kingdom is still incomparably more precious. We consider the soul to be the most precious because, as Macarius the Great said, God was favourably disposed to communicate and to take into His spiritual nature none of the manifested creatures but only man, whom He came to love most of all His creatures. (Macarius the Great, Text on the Freedom of Mind. Ch. 32)

Basil the Great, Gregory the Theologian, John Chrysostom, Cyril of Alexandria, Ambrose of Milan and others preserved their virginity for their entire life which they dedicated to the care for the soul and not for the body. Following their examples, we should care for our soul and nourish the body only for the sake of supporting our spirit. If we, according to our own arbitrariness would exhaust our body so that our spirit would become exhausted also, then such an ascetic deed would be reckless even if it was performed in order to acquire a virtue.

However if God would wish that a man would pass through the ordeal of illnesses then He would also give to that man the patience to endure those illnesses.

Thus let our illnesses come to us not because of our will but from God.

10. With what should one nourish one's soul

If you want to build the house for your soul, Saint Barsanuphius says, then prepare all the necessary materials so that when the painter comes he will need just to accomplish the work. The elements of construction which are necessary for such a building are as follows: the firm faith which is necessary to make the walls; the wooden windows which let the light of the sun illuminate the house so that there will be not even the slightest darkness in it. The wooden windows are the five senses, which are set right by Christ's Holy Cross and let into the house the light of the mental sun of truth which drives out the darkness of your enemy, of the hater of all good.

Then a house needs a roof so that 'The sun shall not smite thee by day, nor the moon by night. (Ps. 121, 6). The roof is kept together by the love for God, which covers the entire house and never falls off and would not let the sun go down while you are still in anger, so that He would not denounce you on the judgment day and sentence you to burn in the fire of hell, and protects you from the moon which testifies about our nightly depression and laziness.

Finally a house needs a door, which lets one in and protects the one who lives in the house. You should understand this as the door in your mind: the Son of God, Who says: 'I am the door.' If you will arrange the house of your soul in such a way and there is nothing in it which could displease God, then He will come with His blessed Father and with the Holy Spirit and He will make His dwelling in your soul and He will teach you the peace of soul and illuminate your heart with an unspeakable joy. (Bars., Letter 171).

It is necessary to nourish the soul with God's word: as Gregory the Theologian says, God's word is the bread of Angels by which the souls which crave for God nourish themselves. Most of all it is necessary to read the New Testament and the Psalter; the Gospels and the letters of the Apostles should be read while standing before the holy icons but the psalms can be read while sitting. Reading the Holy Scripture illuminates the mind and opens Divine possibilities in it. It is necessary to train yourself to have your mind as if swimming in the Lord's Law which should also be the guide line in your way of life. It is very useful to read God's word in solitude and to read the entire Bible in an intelligent way (concentrating on the meaning of it). For such an exercise, besides other good deeds, the Lord will not deprive man of His mercy but He will grant him the gift of understanding. And when man nourishes his soul with God's word, then he receives the insight from God of what is good and what is evil.

The reading of God's word should be done in solitude in order to let the mind of the reader be totally immersed into the truths of the Holy Scripture and to receive from God the warmth which causes tears when the reader is alone. The tears make man's entire being warm and then he receives spiritual gifts which delight the mind and the heart more than any word.

'Physical work and the practice of reading Divine Scripture', Isaac the Syrian teaches, 'guard man's purity, and the physical work is supported by hope and fear. Hope and fear in one's mind are caused in their turn by one's striving for seclusion and incessant prayer. Until man has received the Consoler, he needs Holy Scripture, so that the memory of what is good will become imprinted on his mind and his aspiration for good will be kept active by the incessant reading and it (the aspiration to what is good) will guard man's soul from the passionate ways of sin (fiery temptations). Man needs this because he has not yet acquired the necessary strength of Spirit, which removes delusions, keeps before his eyes recollections which are good for his soul and it is useful when coldness occurs when the mind is distracted. For when the power of the Spirit descends onto the power of the soul which is active in man, then the commandments of the Spirit replace in man's heart the law of the Scriptures and they (the commandments) become rooted there. Then man is instructed secretly by the Spirit and he does not need the help of anything material (as e.g. Scripture). As long as the heart learns through something material then learning is followed by delusion and oblivion. And when the teaching comes from the Spirit then the memory remains intact (Isaac the Syrian, Homily 58).

It is necessary also to nourish the soul with knowledge about the Church, how it came into being and how it was preserved till nowadays and what ordeals it had to go through in different periods of time. It is necessary to know this not to satisfy a wish to govern other people but for the sake of possible inquiries, also for convincing and consoling one's own spirit.

Most of all it is necessary to do this to help oneself to acquire peace of soul, according to the words of the Psalmist: 'Thy peace in abundance comes to those who love Thy law' (Ps. 118, 165).

11. ON PEACE OF SOUL

Peace of soul is obtained by sorrows. Scripture says: 'we went through fire and through water: but thou broughtest us out into a wealthy place.' (Ps. 65, 12) The path of those who wish to please God is littered with many sorrows. How loudly should we praise the holy Martyrs for the suffering that they have undergone for God's sake, while we cannot even stand fever?

Nothing is so favourable to acquire inner peace as one's silence and an incessant conversation with oneself and seldom conversation with others.

And nothing is better than peace in Christ, as it destroys every attack of the aerial and earthly evil spirits. For 'our struggle is not against blood and flesh but against the sources and rulers of the darkness of this century, the spirits of evil.' (Eph. 6, 12)

The sign of one's spiritual life is immersing in oneself and secret work inside one's heart. God's Grace dawns upon such a man and he comes into a peaceful frame of mind and through this he reaches the most peaceful state. A peaceful state comes from a clean conscience, but the most peaceful states comes when man contemplates with his mind the grace of the Holy Spirit inside himself, according to God's word: 'His place is in peace.' (Ps. 75, 3)

Can man not feel joy when he sees the sun with his physical eyes? But it is immeasurably more joyful when the mind sees by its inner eye the Sun of truth, Christ. Then man feels the joy that Angels feel. This is exactly what the Apostle called 'Our life is established in heaven' (Phil. 3, 20).

He who firmly preserves a peaceful temper, extracts, as if with a spoon, spiritual gifts.

The holy fathers lived long as they had a peaceful temper and were shielded by God's grace.

When man acquires a peaceful temper, then he can pour out from himself the light of the illuminated mind also onto others. And until he has acquired such a state, he should keep in mind constantly the following words of Hannah the prophetess: 'let not proud words leave thy mouth' (1 Kings, 2, 3) and the words of the Lord: 'Thou hypocrite, first cast out the beam out of thine own eye; and then shalt thou see clearly to cast out the mote out of thy brother's eye.' (Math. 7, 5)

This is the peace that our Lord Jesus Christ granted His disciples before His death, when He said: 'Peace I leave with you, my peace I give unto you: not as the world giveth, give I unto you.'(Jn. 14, 27). The Apostle (Paul) also mentioned it: 'And the peace of God, which passeth all understanding, shall keep your hearts and minds through Jesus Christ.' (Phil. 4, 7); 'Follow peace with all men, and holiness, without which no man shall see the Lord' (Hebr 12, 14).

Thus we should focus all our thoughts, wishes and actions on acquiring God's peace and call always together with the Church: 'Oh our Lord and God , give us Thy peace' (Is. 26, 12).

12. On preserving peace of soul

It is necessary to try by all means to preserve peace of soul and not to become indignant because of insults. For this one needs to restrain oneself from anger and to pay heed to guard the mind and the heart against improper doubts. One should endure insults indifferently and should train oneself to treat them as if they do not concern one.

This exercise can set our heart at peace and make it a dwelling of God Himself.

We find an example of such mildness in the life of Saint Gregory the Wonderworker. A whore demanded publicly a recompense from him stating that he sinned with her. He was not in the least angry with her, but said meekly to one of his friends: 'give her what she asks without delay.' When the woman received the money she was attacked by a demon. The Saint however drove the demon out from her by prayer. (Lives of the Saints, 17th November).

In case it should be impossible to restrain oneself from becoming indignant, it is necessary at least to restrain one's tongue, according to the words of the Psalmist: 'I am so troubled that I cannot speak.' (Ps. 76, 4).

In this case we can follow the example of Saint Spiridon of Trimithunt and Saint Ephraim the Syrian. Saint Spiridon (Lives of the Saints, 12th December) treated an insult as follows: when he was summoned to come to the Byzantine Emperor, as he was entering the palace, one of the servants who were in the palace thought him a beggar. The servant laughed at him, did not let him come to the emperor and he even hit Saint Spiridon on the cheek. The Saint, as he was mild, turned his other cheek to him, following the words of Christ (Math. 5,39).

When Saint Ephraim the Syrian (Lives of the Saints, 28th January) was once fasting in the desert, he was deprived of his food in the following way: his disciple on his way broke the container. When the Saint saw his disciple, looking sad, he said: 'Do not be upset, brother: if the food did not want to come to us, then we will go to it.' And the

Saint went to the broken vessel and sat down there and ate the rest of the food that he could scrape out of the vessel. Such was his mildness.

And in regard to the way we can conquer our anger, we can learn from the life of Saint Paisius the Great (Lives of the Saints, 19th June). Saint Paisius asked Christ, when He appeared to him, to liberate him from anger. And the Saviour said to him: 'if you want to conquer anger and rage all together, desire nothing, hate nobody and humiliate no one.'

In order to preserve peace of soul it is necessary to drive off despondency and try to have a joyful spirit, following the words of the wise Jesus Sirach: 'I have driven off many sorrows as there is no use in them.' (Eccl., 30, 25)

Also it is necessary for the sake of peace of soul to avoid condemning others. The peace of soul is kept by lenience to others and by silence. When man is in such a state he receives Divine revelations.

In order not to lapse into condemning others man should pay heed to himself, accept from no one the bad thoughts and be as dead to everything.

It is necessary in favour of peace of soul to immerse in oneself often and to ask the question: 'where am I?'

Together with this, it is necessary to observe that the bodily senses, especially the sight, should serve the inner man and should not amuse and distract the soul with material objects. For only those receive the gifts of grace, who are busy with inner work and are watchful in regard of their souls.

13. On feats.

It is not advisable to undertake excessive feats but to do one's best to make our friend – our flesh – loyal and capable of performing virtues.

It is necessary to follow the middle path, 'turn not to the right hand, nor to the left.' (Prv., 4, 27): to give the spirit the spiritual nourishment, and the body – the bodily nourishment, which is needed for the maintenance of this temporary life. One should not reject the lawful demands of the public life, following the words of the Scripture: 'Render therefore unto Caesar the things which are Caesar's; and unto God the things that are God's.' (Math. 22, 21)

One should be lenient towards the weaknesses and imperfections of one's own soul and endure one's own shortcomings as we tolerate the shortcomings of our neighbours, and at the same time not become lazy but impel oneself to work on one's improvement incessantly.

Whether you have eaten too much or you have done something else of this kind, because of the weakness of human nature, do not become indignant, do not add another harm to the harm which has already happened, but impel yourself manly to correct it and at the same time to preserve peace of soul, following the words of the Apostle: 'blessed is he that condemneth not himself ....' (Rom. 14, 22). These words of the Saviour have the same meaning: 'Except ye be converted, and become as little children, ye shall not enter into the kingdom of heaven.' (Math. 18, 3)

A body which is exhausted by labour or illness should be fortified by moderate sleep, food and drink, without even taking into account what time of the day it is. Jesus Christ, immediately after He raised Jairus' daughter from the dead, ' he commanded to give her to eat.' (Lk., 8, 55)

We should refer any success in anything to God and say with the Prophet: 'Not unto us, O Lord, not unto us, but unto thy name give glory' (Ps. 115, 1).

Before the age of 35, that is, the middle of his life, man needs to undertake heroic efforts in order to preserve himself, but many at this age stray off the path of virtues, and become corrupted and follow their own wishes. Saint Basil the Great attests this (Homilies): many have collected a lot in their youth, but when they reached the middle of their life and the cunning spirits attacked them, they could not stand the tumult and lost everything they had collected.

In order not to experience such a transformation, one should examine oneself as one measured by ordeals and pay heed to oneself during one's entire life, following the words of Saint Isaac the Syrian: 'Everyone should weigh his life as if on the scale.' (Homily 40)

14. ON THE LIGHT OF CHRIST

In order to receive and to feel in one's heart the light of Christ, one should draw away one's attention as much as possible from all visible objects. Then, first having purified the soul by repentance and good deeds, and with a sincere faith in the Crucified, one should close one's bodily eyes, immerse the mind in the heart and cry and call incessantly the name of our Lord Jesus Christ. Then, in proportion to the zeal and ardour of spirit towards the Beloved (Lk., 3, 22) man finds in the Name that he is invoking a delight, which will prompt him to search for the highest illumination.

When the mind will stay long in the heart, doing this exercise, then the light of Christ will start to shine and will illuminate the chamber of the soul by Divine light, as God said through His prophet Malachi: 'But unto you that fear My name shall the Sun of righteousness arise' (Mal. 4, 2). This light is at the same time life, according to the words of the Gospel: 'In Him was life; and the life was the light of men.' (Jn., 1, 4).

When man contemplates inwardly the eternal light, then his mind is pure and does not have any material thoughts. It (the mind) becomes completely immersed in the contemplation of uncreated goodness and beauty, it forgets all which is matter and does not even want to see itself but it wishes to hide in the core of the earth just in order not to be deprived of this, the true good: God.

15. ON TEARS

All the holy monks who renounced the world have wept their entire life, hoping for the eternal consolation, as the

Saviour of the world had promised us: 'Blessed are they that mourn: for they shall be comforted.' (Math. 5, 4).

Should we ourselves weep in the same way pleading for forgiveness of our sins? Let the words of the King-Prophet convince us: 'He that goeth forth and weepeth, bearing precious seed, shall doubtless come again with rejoicing, bringing his sheaves with him. ' (Ps. 125, 6). Also the words of Isaac the Syrian: 'make your cheeks wet by your tears so that the Holy Spirit may rest on you and wash from you the foulness of your malice. Win the Lord's grace by your tears, so that He will come to you.' (Homily 68, on renouncing the world.)

When we weep while praying and there comes at the same time laughter, this is the devil's cunning. It is difficult to unmask all the secret and crafty actions of our enemy.

The heart of one who sheds tears of emotion, is illuminated by the rays of the Sun of truth – God Christ.

16. ON REPENTANCE

He who is seeking salvation should always have his heart distressed and inclined to repentance: 'The sacrifices of God are a broken spirit: a broken and a contrite heart, O God, thou wilt not despise' (Ps. 50, 19).

With a distressed spirit man can stand easily and without trouble all the cunning machinations of the devil, who uses all his powers with the aim to confuse man's spirit and to sow his tares through this confusion, as the Gospel tells us. 'He said unto them, an enemy hath done this.' (Math. 13, 28).

When man, on the contrary, tries to be humble of heart and to preserve a peaceful state of mind then all the enemy's machinations are in vain. For where the thoughts are peaceful, there God abides; it is said 'His dwelling is in peace.' (Ps. 75, 3)

The initial point of repentance is fear of God and heedfulness, as the holy martyr Boniface (Lives of the Saints, 19th December) says: the fear of God is the father of heedfulness, and heedfulness is the mother of inner peace. The fear of God awakens the sleeping conscience, and the conscience makes the soul see its ugliness as if in the mirror of a pure and unstirred water. This is how are born and grow still deeper the roots of repentance.

We insult God's greatness during our entire life by our sins and therefore we should humbly ask the Lord to forgive us our debts.

Is it possible for one who has received God's grace but has fallen, to rise up again through repentance?

It is possible, according to the Psalmist: 'Thou hast thrust sore at me that I might fall: but the Lord helped me.'

(Ps. 117, 13). When the holy prophet Nathan pointed out to David his sin, then David repented and was immediately forgiven.

Another example to illustrate this is the story of the anchorite who went to fetch water at a spring and lapsed into sin there. Having returned to his cell, he realized that he has sinned and he started again leading an ascetic life as before. The enemy (devil) tried to confuse him, stressing the heaviness of his sin, trying to convince him that he would not be forgiven and trying to lead him astray from the ascetic life. But Christ's warrior stood his ground firmly and remained on the ascetic path. God revealed this event to a certain holy father and ordered him to glorify the brother who sinned, for such a victory over the devil.

When we repent sincerely of our sins and appeal to our Lord Jesus Christ with all our heart, then He rejoices with us. He makes a feast and invites to this feast all His favourite Forces and shows them the 'drachma, that He found again: that is His royal image and likeness. He puts on His shoulders the lost sheep and brings it to His Father. God abides again in the house of joy, the soul of the repented one, together with the souls which never turned away from Him.

Thus let us not be careless and let us turn to our merciful Lord without delay and not lapse into carelessness and despair because of our sins. For our despair is a perfect joy to the devil. It is a deadly sin, as the Scripture says. (1 Jn. 5, 16. Anthony, Text 77). 'If you will not surrender to despondency and negligence,' saint Barsanuphius says, 'then you will witness the wonder and you will praise God as He will change you from a sinner into a righteous one.' (Letter 114).

To repent of a sin means amongst other things not to commit this sin again.

As there is a particular remedy for any decease, there is repentance for every sin. Thus start repenting without doubts and your repentance will plead for you before God. Pray incessantly the following prayer of Saint Antioch: 'Knowing Thy infinite mercy, oh Lord, I dare to bring forth to Thee out of my foul mouth this prayer: remember that Thy holy name came over me and that Thou redeemed me at the cost of Thy blood, that you established me by the betrothal of Thy Holy Spirit and raised me from the abyss of my unlawful deeds not to let the enemy rob me. Jesus Christ, protect me and be my strong helper in the battle as I am the slave of lust and it wages war against me. Oh Lord, do not leave me fallen on the ground condemned by my own deeds: free me, oh Lord, of the cunning slavery of the prince of this world and make me follow Thy commandments. Thou art my life and my path and Thy countenance is light for my eyes, oh Lord and God. Do not let me look boldly and haughtily and relieve me from evil lust: protect me by Thy holy hand. Do not let my wants and lusts deceive me and do not commit me to the shameless soul. Let the light of Thy countenance shine on me so that the darkness will not seize me and those who walk in darkness will not steal me. Do not hand over, oh Lord, the soul which confesses Thee to the invisible beasts. Do not let Thy servant, oh Lord, be wounded by the enemy's dogs. Make me the receptacle of the Thy Holy Spirit and make me the house of Thy Christ, oh Holy Father. Oh Thee, guide of the lost ones, guide me so that I will not go astray to the left. I long to see Thy countenance, oh Lord. Oh God, guide me by the light of Thy countenance. Give me, Thy servant, the source of tears, and give me, Thy creature, the dew of Thy Holy Spirit, so that I will not wither like the fig-tree that Thou cursed. Let my tears be my drink and my prayers be my food. Turn, oh Lord, my weeping into joy and accept me into Thy eternal dwellings. Let Thy grace, oh Lord, come onto me, and let Thy generous gifts fill me and forgive me all my sins. Thou art the true God, Who forgives unlawful deeds. And do not let the work of Thy hands be harmed because of the multitude of my unlawful deeds, but summon me to rise up through Thy only Son, our Saviour. And save me, who lies in sickness, as Thou saved Levi the publican, and revive me, killed by my own sins, as Thou revived the son of the widow. As Thou art the only resurrection of the dead and Thou art praised in the ages of ages. Amen. (Antioch, Homily 77).

17. ON FASTING

Fasting means not only to eat seldom, but also to eat little; and it does not mean to eat once a day only, but it means not to eat much. He who is fasting is not reasonable if he only eats at a certain time, but during the meal is totally committed with his mind and body to the process of eating. It is also necessary not to be concerned whether the food is tasty or not. This concern, which is appropriate to animals, is not to be praised in a man of reason. We reject tasty food in order to tame the rebelling parts of our flesh and to give to our spirit freedom to act.

True fasting means not only exhaustion of the flesh, but it means also to give part of the bread that you wanted to eat yourself, to one who hungers for it. 'Blessed are they which do hunger and thirst after righteousness: for they shall be filled.' (Math. 5, 6).

The founder of the feat and our Saviour the Lord Jesus Christ, before He undertook the heroic deed of redemption of the human race, fortified Himself by a long period of fasting. And all the ascetics, when starting work for God, armed themselves by fasting and walked on the path of the cross during the feat of fasting only. They even considered the measure of their success in the ascetic practises by their success in fasting.

Saints have learnt strict fasting not at once, but trained themselves gradually and little by little to be content with the poorest meal. Saint Dorotheus, while training his disciple Dositheus in fasting, gradually reduced Dositheus' daily portion of 1,6 kg, so that it finally became one hundred grams of bread.

In this way the holy fasters, to the great surprise of people around, were not weakened, but they were always vigilant, strong and ready for action. They were seldom ill and their life was extremely long.

In proportion to the growing fineness and lightness of the flesh of the faster, his spiritual life becomes still more perfect and reveals itself by miraculous appearances. The spirit manifests itself as if not in a physical body. The physical senses become shut off and the mind, having detached itself from the earth, ascends to heaven and immerses itself in the contemplation of the spiritual world. Not everyone however can impose on himself a severe rule of abstinence, or deprive himself of all that could support him in his shortcomings. 'All men cannot receive this saying, save they to whom it is given.' (Math. 19, 12).

It is necessary to consume daily the right amount of food which is needed for the body to be strong enough to be the friend and the helper of the soul in performing the virtues. Otherwise it might happen that if the body gets weak then the soul will weaken also. Follow the example of the (holy) Fathers and during the four periods of fasting of the year, eat a meal on Wednesdays and Fridays only once a day. Then the angel of God will be with you always.

18. ON GUARDING THE MIND

We should incessantly guard our heart from indecent thoughts and impressions, following the words in Proverbs

'Keep thy heart with all diligence; for out of it are the issues of life' (Prvb. 4, 23)
If the heart is guarded vigilantly then purity is born in it, which can contemplate God, as the eternal Truth promises us: 'Blessed are the pure in heart: for they shall see God.' (Math., 5, 8).
We should not expose what is best kept inside our heart without necessity. Only then is what we have gathered secured against the visible and invisible enemies, when it is preserved like a treasure inside the heart. Do not open to all and everyone the secrets of your heart.

19. ON VERBOSITY

Verbosity alone with those whose disposition is opposite to ours would be enough to upset the inner mood of the mindful man.
But the most regretful of all is that it (verbosity) can extinguish that very fire that our Lord Jesus Christ came to cast into the ground of human hearts. Nothing cools so quickly the fire, which the Holy Spirit blows into the heart of the monk for the sanctification of his soul, as personal contacts with others and verbose conversations with them. Exceptions are contacts with children about God's mysteries, for the sake of obtaining knowledge of Him and coming closer to Him. (Isaac the Syrian, Homily 8)
A monk should most of all restrain himself from contacting women. As a wax candle, even unlit, will melt when put between burning candles, so the monk's heart will become weaker from contacts with women. Saint Isidore of Pelusion says: 'what are the bad talks which corrupt good customs? This is conversing with women. Even if it would be done for a good reason still it can corrupt strongly, in a secret way, our inner man, and even if the body would remain pure, the soul would be corrupted. What is harder than a stone? What is softer than water? However, a constant effort conquers nature. If the nature of a stone, which is hardly changeable, is liable to destruction by water, which seems

nothing in comparison to the stone, then how could man's will, which can be influenced easily, not be conquered and manipulated by a long-lasting pressure?' (Saint Isidore of Pelusion, Lives of the Saints, 4th February, letter 284.)

Therefore one needs to restrain one's tongue from verbosity for the sake of protecting the inner man. 'The wise man keeps silence' (Prvb. 11, 12) 'The one who controls his mouth, preserves his soul' (13, 3) and remembering the words of Job: 'I made a covenant with mine eyes, why then should I look upon a maid' (31, 1) and the words of the Lord Jesus Christ: 'Whosoever looketh on a woman to lust after her, hath committed adultery with her already in his heart' (Math. 5, 28)

One should not speak before one has listened to what one's collocutor has to say: 'He that answereth a matter before he heareth it, it is folly and shame unto him' (Prvb. 18, 13).

20. On discernment of what is in the heart

When man receives something from God, his heart rejoices; when man receives something from the devil, he gets confused.

A Christian heart, having received something from God, does not need an external proof that it came from the Lord, as by the effect of God's message it is convinced that it is a heavenly gift, as the heart feels such spiritual fruits as 'love, joy, peace, longsuffering, mercy, faith, meekness.' (Glt. 5, 22)

As regards the devil, on the contrary even if he would present himself as the 'angel of light' (2 Cor. 11, 14) or would suggest the most specious thoughts, the heart will still feel some unclearness, confusion in its thoughts and feelings. Saint Macarios the Egyptian explains it as follows: 'even though the devil would produce visions of light, he cannot inspire good deeds, which is the way to recognize his tricks.' (Homily 4, ch. 13)

Thus through various feelings which arise in the heart man can learn to recognize what is of God, and what is of the devil. Gregory the Sinaite writes about its as follows: 'by its effect on you, you can recognize whether the light which appeared in your soul is from God or from the devil.' (Philokalia, part 1, Gregory the Sinaite 'On silence')

21. ON ILLNESSES

The body is the slave, while the soul is the sovereign. Therefore it often happens that by God's mercy the body becomes exhausted by illnesses and the passions become weaker. As the result of this one comes to one's senses. In addition, an illness itself is sometimes caused by some passion or other.

Remove sin and there will be no more illnesses : they affect us because of our sins, as Saint Basil the Great states. 'Where does the disease come from? What causes the injuries of the body? The Lord created the body, not the disease; He created the soul and not the sin. What is then the most useful and necessary thing for us? Union with God and contact with Him through love. When we lose this love we fall away from Him, and when we have fallen away from Him, we undergo various and divers diseases (On the notion that God is not the cause of evil, page 213).

If one endures one's illness patiently and gratefully, then it is regarded to him as a feat, and even more than a feat.

An elder who suffered from dropsy, said once to his brethren who visited him having a wish to apply to him one or another medical treatment: 'I beseech you, fathers, to pray for my inner man, so that he would not undergo such an illness. With regard to my physical suffering I pray to God that He would not free me from it too soon, for 'though our outer man perish, yet the inner man is renewed.' (2 Cor. 4, 16)

22. ON ALMSGIVING

Man should be merciful to beggars and wanderers: the great luminaries and Fathers of the Church have cared much about this. In regard to this virtue we should try by all means to observe God's following commandment: 'be ye therefore merciful as your Father also is merciful' (Lk. 6, 36) and also: 'I will have mercy, and not sacrifice'. (Math. 9, 13)

The wise ones pay heed to these words, while the unwise do not. This is the reason why their reward is unequal, exactly as it is said: 'He which soweth sparingly shall reap also sparingly; and he which soweth bountifully shall reap also bountifully.' (2 Cor., 9, 6).

Let the example of Peter the Bread Giver (Lives of the Saints, 22nd September), all whose sins were forgiven, as it was shown to him in a vision, inspire us to be merciful to our neighbours for even the little alms help acquire the kingdom of heaven.

We must give alms while at the same time showing our good disposition to the person, following the teaching of Saint Isaac the Syrian: 'when you give something to one in need, let your act be preceded by the joyfulness of your face and the good words which console his grief.' (Homily 89.)

23. ON THOUGHTS AND IMPULSES OF THE FLESH

We should try to keep ourselves free from impure thoughts, especially, when we pray to God. For there is no unity between stench and fragrance.

For this one should ward off an attack of sinful thoughts and impulses at the very beginning and uproot them out from our heart. While the 'children of Babylon', that is the evil impulses and thoughts, are still 'babies', one should crush them on the stone which is Christ. Most of all man ought to crush the three following passions: gluttony, the passion for money and vanity. By these three passions the devil tried to seduce even our Lord Jesus Christ at the end of His ascetic feats in the desert.

The devil, hiding like a lion in his den (Ps. 9, 30), sets for us his secret traps of impure and impious thoughts.

Therefore when we discover them we should immediately destroy them by the means of pious thoughts and prayer. One needs great watchfulness and heroic efforts in order to keep one's mind in unison with one's heart and words, so that the praise of our prayer would not become mixed with stench. For the Lord has an aversion for a heart with unclean thoughts. The law says: 'thou shalt not plough with an ox and an ass together' (Deut., 22, 10) that is do not pray with clean and unclean thoughts together.

Let us follow the example of David who says: 'I will early destroy all the wicked of the land, that I may cut off all wicked doers from the city of the Lord.' (Ps. 100, 8). The law forbade

an unclean person to enter the house of the Lord. We ourselves are the house of the Lord, and Jerusalem lies within us. The 'wicked of the land' are the serpent-like thoughts which lurk in our heart. Let us then also appeal together with David to the Lord: 'rescue my soul from their destructions' (Ps. 34, 17); 'scatter thou the people that delight in war' (Ps. 67, 31) so that also we could hear 'Thou calledst in trouble, and I delivered thee.' (Psalm 80, 8).

Let us throw ourselves weeping incessantly, day and night, before God's goodness, so that He will purify our hearts from any evil thought, and we can follow the path of our calling and bring to Him the gifts of our service with clean hands.

When we do not agree with evil thoughts that the devil induces in us, then we do a good thing.

The evil spirit has influence only on the passionate; to those who purified themselves from the passions he sticks on to only externally.

It is impossible at a young age not to be disturbed by the impulses of the flesh. But one ought to pray to God asking that the spark of vicious passions would be extinct at the very beginning. Then the fire will not flare up.

24. On patience and humility

For the sake of God man should endure anything that happens to him with gratitude.

Our life lasts a minute in comparison with eternity and therefore 'the sufferings of this present time', according to the Apostle, 'are not worthy to be compared with the glory which shall be revealed to us'. (Rom. 8, 18)

When the enemy insults you, endure it silently and then open your heart only to God.

If someone humiliates or dishonours you, try by all means to forgive him, following the words of the Gospel: 'of him that taketh away thy goods, ask them not again' (Luke 6, 30).

When people abuse us we should consider ourselves unworthy of praise, assuming that if we would be worthy of it then everybody would bow for us.

We should always humiliate ourselves before everyone, following the teaching of Saint Isaac the Syrian: 'humiliate yourself and then you will see God's glory inside you.'

Thus let us love humility and let us witness God's glory: there where humility comes from, there is also God's glory. If there is no light, then there is only darkness; when there is no humility in man then there is nothing but darkness in him.

As the wax which is not warmed up and not softened, cannot be imprinted with a seal which is pressed to it, so the soul which was not tested by labour and sicknesses, cannot receive the seal of God's virtue. When the devil fell back from the Lord, then the Angels approached Him and served Him. (Math. 4, 11) In the same way, when in the time of our temptation God's Angels withdraw from us, they do not withdraw far, and they come back soon and serve us by inducing in us Divine thoughts, tenderness, delight, patience. The soul, having done its work, acquires also other virtues. That is why the holy Prophet Isaiah says: 'they that wait upon the Lord shall renew their strength; they shall mount up with wings as eagles; they shall run and not be weary; and they shall walk and not faint.' (Is. 40, 31)

The meek David had also to endure in such a way: when Shimei abused him and threw stones at him, saying: 'Go away, thou bloody man', David did not become angry. When Abishai became indignant with this and said to David: 'why should this dead dog curse my lord the King?', David stopped him, saying: 'Let him alone and let him curse, ... the Lord will look on mine affliction and the Lord will requite me good.' (2 Kings, 16, 7-12). That is why he later sang : 'I waited patiently for the Lord and He inclined unto me, and heard my cry.' (Ps. 39, 2)

'The furnace proveth the potter's vessels; so the trial of man is in his reasoning.'

(Eccl. 27, 5). 'Woe unto you that have lost patience! What will ye do when the Lord shall visit you?' (Eccl. 2, 14)

As a father who loves his children, when he sees that his son lives disorderly, punishes him; and when he sees that his son is weak and hardly endures punishment, he consoles him, so our good Lord and Father treats us because of His love for us, applying, for our improvement, consolations as well as punishments. Therefore when we are in sorrow, we, as obedient children, striving for good, should thank God. For if we would thank Him only when we are in prosperity, we will be similar to ungrateful Jews, who having been satiated by the wonder of food in the desert, said that Christ is a true prophet and wanted to make Him a king; however, when He said to them: 'eat not the perishable food but the food which leads you to eternal life', they asked Him: 'Where is your miracle? Our fathers ate manna in the desert.' It is exactly them of whom the word of the psalm speaks: 'he shall give thanks to Thee when Thou doest well to him,' and such one 'will never see the light.' (Ps. 48, 19, 20)

Therefore the apostle Jacob teaches us: 'My brethren, count it all joy when ye fall into divers temptations; Knowing this that the trying of your faith worketh patience, but let patience have her perfect work that ye may be perfect and entire.' And he adds to it: 'blessed is the man that endureth temptation; for when he is tried, he shall receive the crown of life.' (Jac. I, 2-4, 12)

25. On duties and love for one's neighbours

Man should treat his neighbours gently, without even the slightest insult.

When we turn away from somebody or insult him, then a heaviness like a stone appears in our heart.

The spirit of a confused or a depressed man should be encouraged with the word of love. If your brother sins, then cover him, following the advice of Saint Isaac the Syrian (Homily 89): 'Spread your garment over the sinner and cover him.'

We all are in need of God's mercy, as the Church sings: 'Had the Lord not been in us, who would have been preserved whole from the enemy, and likewise from the murderer of man.' We should be in regard to our neighbours, pure in our words and thoughts, and treat all equally, otherwise our life is in vain.

We should love our neighbours not less than ourselves, according to the words of the Lord: 'love thy neighbour as thyself'. (Lk. 10, 27) However love for our neighbour should not exceed the limits of moderation and divert us from obeying the first and foremost commandment: love for God, as our Lord Jesus Christ teaches us: 'He that loveth father or mother more than Me is not worthy of Me; and he that loveth son or daughter more than me is not worthy of me.' (Math. 10, 37)

We find a good elaboration of this topic in Saint Dimitri of Rostov (Part 2, admonition 2): 'an untrue love towards God in a Christian is when the creature is put on the same level as the Creator; and the true love is when the Creator is loved and preferred above the entire creation.'

26. On not condemning one's neighbour and on forgiveness of insults

Man should judge no one, even if with his own eyes he saw someone sinning or living in transgression of the Lord's commandments, following God's words: 'Judge not so that ye be not judged' (Math. 7, 1); 'who art thou, that judgest another man's servant? To his own master he standeth or faileth, he shall be holden up for God is able to make him stand.' (Rom. 14, 4)

It is much better to recall the following word of the Apostle: 'Wherefore let him that thinketh he standeth take heed lest he fall.' (I Cor. 10, 12)

For it is not known to us how long we can hold our ground in preserving our virtues. As the Prophet says from his own experience: 'In my prosperity I said: I shall never be moved. But thou didst hide Thy face, I was troubled.' (Ps. 29, 7, 8)

One should not try to revenge an offence, no matter how hard it was, but on the contrary, to forgive your offender wholeheartedly even though the heart would resist it. One should try to convince one's heart with the following words of God: 'But if ye forgive not men their trespasses, neither will your heavenly Father forgive your trespasses.' (Math. 6, 15); 'pray for them which despitefully use you and persecute you.' (Math. 5, 44)

One oughtn't to coddle anger or hate in one's heart towards one's neighbour who is at enmity with one, but on the contrary, love him, and, where possible, do good to him, following the teaching of our Lord Jesus Christ: 'love your enemies and do good to them that hate you.' (Math. 5, 44)

Thus if we will try to fulfil all this, according to the measure of our strength, then we may hope that the Divine light, which illuminates the path to the heavenly Jerusalem, will shine in our hearts.

Let us follow the example of those who were God's beloved: let us follow the example of the meek David, about whom the most good and good-loving God said: 'I found a man to My liking, who will fulfil all My wishes.' Thus spoke He about David, who was without rancour and forgiving, who was kind towards his enemies. And we will not revenge ourselves on our brothers, so that, as it is said by Saint Antioch, 'we would not have pauses during prayer.' The law commands to take care of the enemy's donkey. (Exodus 23, 5). God mentioned Job as a mild, forgiving man. Josef did not revenge himself on his brothers, who caused so much trouble for him. Abel went along with his brother Cain, trustfully and without suspicion. According to the testimony of the Scriptures, all the saints lived without anger. Jeremiah, conversing with God (Jer. 18, 20) says about Israel which persecuted him: 'Shall evil be recompensed for good? Remember that I stood before Thee to speak good for them.' (Antioch, Discourse 52). God commanded to be at enmity only with the snake, that is with the one who seduced man at the beginning of time and caused his banishment from paradise, with the murderer of man, the devil. Also, it is commanded to us to be at enmity with the Midianites, that is the evil spirits of lust and shamelessness which sow in the heart the unclean and nasty thoughts. The most perfect virtue and wisdom is the ingenuous artless acting in accordance with the reason. Why do we condemn our brethren? It is because we do not make efforts to become fully aware of ourselves. He who is busy with checking himself does not have time to watch others. Condemn yourself and you will cease condemning others.

Condemn the bad deed, and do not condemn the person who did it.

We ought to consider ourselves the most sinful of all, and forgive our neighbour for any of his bad deeds, and we should hate only the devil, who seduced our neighbour. It happens also that it seems to us that someone does things in a wrong way, while, because of his good intention it is in fact, a good deed. Besides, the door of repentance is open to all and it is not certain, who will enter this door first: you who condemn, or the one whom you condemn.

If you condemned your neighbour, Saint Antioch teaches that then you are condemned at the same time exactly for the same sin. It is not required from us to judge or to condemn, but only God can judge, as only He knows our hearts and the innermost passions of our nature (Antioch, Word 49).

Thus, my beloved ones, let us not watch the sins of others and condemn them, in order to spare us hearing the words: 'the sons of men, their teeth are spears and arrows, and their tongue is a sharp sword.' (Ps. 56, 5)

For when the Lord will leave man to his own resources then the devil is there, ready to grind him like a mill grinds the grain.

27. Against excessive care

Excessive care for worldly things is caused by lack of faith and faintheartedness. Woe unto us, if we, caring for ourselves, do not become firmly established in our hope in God, Who cares for us. If we do not ascribe to Him the visible good that we use in this temporary life, how can we expect from Him the good, which is promised to us in the future eternal life. Let us not be such sceptics, but let us better 'seek first the Kingdom of God, and all these things shall be added' (Math. 6, 33), according to the word of the Saviour. It is better for us to despise what is not ours, that is the temporary and corruptible; and to long for what is ours, the incorruptible and immortal. For when we will become incorruptible and immortal then we will be awarded the visible contemplation of God, like the Apostles, who saw the Divine Transfiguration. We will reach unity with God, which is beyond any comprehension, like the heavenly minds (heavenly hierarchies). For we will be equal unto the Angels, and 'are the children of God, being the children of the resurrection.' (Lk. 20, 36)

'There is a disease,' Ecclesiast says, 'I saw it under the sun, the abundance of the rich will not suffer him to sleep; and those riches perish by evil travail. And all his days he eateth in darkness, and he hath much sorrow and wrath with his sickness.' (Eccl. 5, 12, 16)

28. ON SADNESS

When the evil spirit of sadness has seized a soul, then it fills it with its bitterness and troubles, and in this way does not allow the soul to pray with appropriate zeal; to read the Holy Scripture with the necessary attention. It deprives the soul of meekness and placidity in its communication with brethren and causes unwillingness for any contact with them. For the soul which is full of sadness becomes mad and frenzied and can neither accept a good advice quietly nor answer meekly to the questions put to it. Such a soul runs away from people, as if they are the cause of its confusion, because it does not understand that the cause of illness lies within itself.

A sad monk does not prompt his mind to contemplate and he can never offer a pure prayer.

The one who overcame his passions, at the same time overcame his sadness. However the one who is conquered by his passions will not be able to avoid the fetters of sadness. As an illness can be seen in the colour of the skin of the face, he who is possessed by passion is exposed by his sadness.

He who loves the world, cannot be free from sadness. And he, who despises the world is always joyful.

As fire purifies gold, so the longing for God, and sadness because of His absence purifies a sinful heart. (St Antioch, Discourse 26)

29. ON DESPAIR

According to the teaching of Saint John of the Ladder, a feeling of despair can be caused by two reasons.

The first kind of despair is caused by the awareness of many sins, by the despair of conscience and unbearable sadness. Such a soul, which is covered by many sores, drowns, because of the unbearable pain which is caused by these sores, in the depth of despair.

The second kind of despair is caused by pride and arrogance, when a person considers himself not to deserve the sin into which he has lapsed.

The first kind of despair lures man to commit all kinds of vices indiscriminately, while by the second kind of despair man still holds on to his ascetic practice, which is, John of the Ladder adds, against reason.

The first kind of despair is healed by abstinence and hope on God, and the second kind is healed by humility and restraining from condemning one's neighbours. (The Ladder, 26th rung).

The Lord cares about our salvation. But the devil, man's murderer, tries constantly to drive us to despair.

A soul, which is elevated and firm, does not fall into despair, no matter what troubles come over it. Judas the traitor was faint-hearted and not skilful in struggle. Therefore when the enemy saw Judas' despair, he attacked him and managed to tempt him to hang himself. Peter, on the contrary, the solid rock, when he lapsed into sin, as he was skilful in battle, did not despair and did not lose his spirits. Peter shed bitter tears from the depth of his heart, and these tears scorched the eyes of the enemy, and the enemy ran far away from him screaming in pain.

Thus, brethren, as Saint Antioch teaches, when despair attacks us, let us not give in to it, but let us strengthen and guard ourselves by the light of faith, and let us say manly to the deceitful spirit: "what do we have in common, you, alienated from God, a fugitive from heaven and a deceitful servant. You will not be able to cause us any harm. Christ, the Son of God, has power over us and over everything. We sinned as we broke His commandments and we will repent before Him and will receive His forgiveness. And you, the pernicious one, go away from us. Fortified by Christ's Holy Cross, we trample upon your snake's head.' (Antioch, Discourse 27).

And we will pray with emotion to the Lord: 'Oh Lord God of heaven and earth, King of aeons! In Thy loving kindness, open the door of repentance to me, for I, being ill in my heart, plead Thee, the true God, the Father of our Lord Jesus Christ, the light of the world: take care of me by Thy abundant goodness and accept my prayer; do not reject it, but forgive me as I lapsed into many sins. Bend Thy ear towards my pleading and forgive me all my evil acts, as I was seized by my arbitrariness. For I seek rest and I cannot find it as my conscience does not forgive me. I wait for peace but there is no peace in me because of the great number of my unlawful acts. Hear oh God my heart, which is crying to Thee, do not consider my evil acts, but take care of the illness of my soul and hurry to heal my terrible wounds. Give me time for repentance for the sake of Thy graceful love for man and save me from my disgraceful acts and do not measure me according to Thy truth and do not reward me according to my deeds as I will then completely perish. Oh Lord, hear me, seized by despair. For I am deprived of any preparedness and of any thought of improving myself, and I prostrate myself before thy generous gifts: have mercy on me, as I am thrown down to earth and condemned for my sins. Summon me again, oh Lord and Master, as I am imprisoned and as if fettered by my evil acts. For it is only Thee who can free the prisoners and heal the wounds which are known to no one but Thee, as Thee knoweth the innermost secrets. And that is why I, with all my evil diseases, call only on Thee as Thou art the doctor of all who suffer, the door for all those who weep outside, the path for all those who are lost, the light for those in darkness, the redeemer of prisoners. Thou always keepeth Thy hand at rest and Thou restraineth always Thy anger, meant for sinners, because of Thy great love for man, thou granteth time for repentance to us. Let the light of Thy countenance shine on me, oh my Lord and Master, as I fell deeply and Thou art quick in giving mercy and slow in punishing. Hold out Thy hand for the sake of Thy goodness and erect me from the ditch of my unlawful acts.

As it is only Thee our Lord, Who does not enjoy the death of sinners and Who does not turn away His countenance from those who pray with tears. Hear oh Lord the voice of Thy servant, who cries to Thee, and let Thy light shine on me, who is deprived of light, and grant me Thy grace, so that I, who have no hope, would always hope on Thy help and strength. 'Turn oh Lord my weeping into joy, thou hast put off my sackcloth, and girded me with gladness' (Psalm 29,12). And have the kindness to let me have rest from my evening pursuits and let me find the morning peace of Thy chosen ones, who are free from disease, sadness and crying, and let the door of Thy kingdom open for me so that I may enter it with those who enjoy the light of Thy countenance and receive the eternal life in our Lord Jesus Christ. Amen.'

30. On the reasons why Jesus Christ came into the world

These are the reasons why Jesus Christ, the Son of God came into the world:

1. God's love for the human race: 'God loved the world so much that He gave His only-begotten Son' (Jn. 3, 16)
2. The restoration of the image and likeness of God in fallen man, as the holy Church sings (the 1st canon for the Nativity of Christ, the 1st song): 'Man who, being made in the image of God, had become corrupt through sin, and was full of vileness, and had fallen away from the better life Divine, doth the wise Creator restore anew.'
3. The salvation of human souls: 'For God sent not His Son into the world to condemn the world, but that the world through Him might be saved.' (Jn. 3, 17)

Thus, following the purpose of our Redeemer, the Lord Jesus Christ, we should live according to His Divine teaching, in order to acquire through this the salvation of our souls.

31. On the active and the contemplative life

Man consists of soul and body and therefore the path of his life should consist of actions of the body and the soul, of acts and contemplation.

The path of the active life consists of fasting, abstinence, vigil, kneeling, prayer and other bodily feats, which form together the 'narrow and sorrowful path' which, according to God's word 'leads to eternal life' (Math, 7, 14).

The path of the contemplative life consists of concentrating and elevating the mind towards the Lord God, watchfulness of the heart, inner prayer and contemplation of the spiritual reality, which is induced by the above mentioned exercises.

Anyone who wishes to live the spiritual life should begin with the active life and after that come into the contemplative life for it is impossible to enter the contemplative life without the active life.

The active life serves the purpose of cleansing us from the sinful passions and elevates us to the perfection of acts. By this the active life paves the way for us for a contemplative life. For only those who cleansed themselves from passions and became perfect can lead a contemplative life, as it can be seen from the words of the Holy Scripture: 'blessed are the pure of heart as they shall see God' (Math. 5,8) and from the words of Gregory the Theologian: 'only the perfect can begin with contemplation safely.'

In the same way the Church sings, praising Saint Nicolas: 'first in silence struggling with the thoughts, thou then added the memory of God to thy works. Through thinking of God thou acquired a perfect mind, by which thou conversed boldly with God and the Angels (Akathist to Saint Nicolas, kondakion 10).

Man should begin the contemplative life with fear and trembling, keeping the heart in contrition and humility, after much study of the Holy Scripture. It is better to do it under the guidance of an experienced and skilful starets (elder, spiritual mentor), if one can find him, and not boldly and with self- will.

A bold and ambitious person, according to the words of Saint Gregory the Sinaite (On temptation and many other delusions. Philokalia, part 1), would seek for things of which he is not worthy, and he would proudly try to acquire them prematurely. And also: if someone tries to obtain something high, which is in fact, the devil's wish, and not to find the truth, then such a person is easily trapped by the devil's nets, as one of his own.

In case one cannot find a mentor to guide one towards the contemplative life, then one should follow Holy Scripture, as the Lord Himself commands us to learn from Holy Scripture: 'Search the Scriptures for in them ye think ye have eternal life.' (Jn. 5, 39).

It is necessary also to study diligently the works of the holy fathers and to make efforts, according to one's capacity, to observe what these writings teach. In this way one gradually will ascend from the active life to the perfection of the contemplative life.

For, according to the words of Gregory the Theologian (Homily on the Resurrection) it is the best when every one of us reaches perfection by himself and brings to God, who is calling for us, a sacrifice, which is live, holy and blessed always and everywhere.

The active life should not abandon even if he succeeded in it and reached the contemplative life as the active life stimulates and elevates the contemplative life.

If a monk follows the path of inner, contemplative life, he must not weaken and stray off this path only because most people are attached to the outer, materialistic world and would strike him right in the core of his heart by their opposite views. Such people always try to lead us astray from the inner path, creating various obstacles for us, but we should not give in to this because, according to the opinion of the Teachers of the Church (Comments of Saint Theodoret on the Song of Songs), the contemplation of spiritual things is above the cognition of material things.

Therefore we should not falter over any obstacle on this path, strengthening ourselves with God's word: 'But let us not fear their fear, neither let us be dismayed for God is with us. Let us sanctify the Lord God Himself in heartfelt remembrance of His divine name and fulfilment of His will, and He shall be our fear.' (Is. 8, 12, 13)

***

The Teaching of Saint Seraphim

Staretz Seraphim's cloak, hat and cowl.